Wealth Of Nations

Vietnam

Cath Senker

HODDER
Wayland

an imprint of Hodder Children's Books

Wealth Of Nations series includes:

Brazil	India
China	Malaysia
Egypt	Vietnam

Cover: Main photo: Farmworkers in front of the No Mon Gate Citadel, Hue.
Inset: A woman wearing a traditional hat in Hô Chi Minh City.

Title page: This type of hat is worn by many women in Vietnam.

Contents page: Rush hour in Hô Chi Minh City.

Vietnam is a simplified and updated version of the title in
Hodder Wayland's Economically Developing Countries series.

Text copyright © 2001 Hodder Wayland
Volume copyright © 2001 Hodder Wayland

Editor: Polly Goodman
Language consultant: Norah Granger, Senior Lecturer in Education Studies,
Department of Education, University of Brighton.

First published in Great Britain in 1996 by Wayland Publishers Ltd. This edition updated
and published in 2001 by Hodder Wayland, an imprint of Hodder Children's Books.

British Library Cataloguing in Publication Data
Senker, Cath
   Vietnam. - (Wealth of Nations)
   1. Vietnam - Economic conditions - 20th century - Juvenile literature
   2. Vietnam - Social conditions - 20th century - Juvenile literature
   3. Vietnam - Geography - Juvenile literature
   I. Title
   959.7'044

ISBN 0 7502 3531 4

Printed and bound in Italy by G. Canale & C.S.p.A., Turin.

Hodder Children's Books
A division of Hodder Headline Limited
338 Euston Road, London NW1 3BH

Picture acknowledgements
All photographs are by Ole Steen Hansen, except for: Axiom *Cover (inset)*/Jim Holmes; James
Davis Travel Photography *Cover (main);* Eye Ubiquitous/Tim Page 18 (inset), 19; Topham 15.
All artwork is by Peter Bull.

CONTENTS

'IT'S BETTER NOW'

In Vietnam, people often say, 'It's better now' when they talk about life now compared to the past. For much of its history, Vietnam was ruled by other countries.

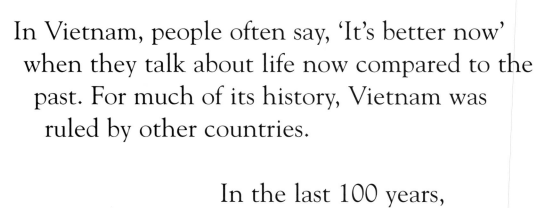

In the last 100 years, France, Japan and the USA have taken over all or parts of Vietnam, one after the other. The war with the USA from 1964 to 1975 was the last chapter in Vietnam's struggle for independence.

◄ A woman holds a flag to celebrate the victory over the war with the USA, in 1975.

◄ Shopping in Cholon, the Chinese part of Hô Chi Minh City.

The war with the USA left Vietnam one of the poorest countries in the world. From 1979 to 1992, Vietnam was given no help from abroad, except from Communist countries. Even with these difficulties, in the 1990s Vietnam's economy grew rapidly as modern industry and business developed. Huge changes are happening in Vietnam.

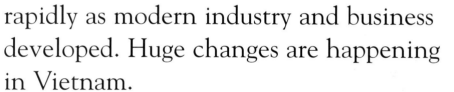

'My family fled from Vietnam when I was very small. When I was 21 years old, I went back to study art in Hanoi. Everything was so different from Canada, where I grew up. The people are so friendly here.' – Mai Phan, a Vietnamese-Canadian.

LAND AND CLIMATE

Vietnam is a beautiful land, with rivers, paddy fields and mountains. It is a long, narrow country, which is about the same area as Italy. It is 1,650 kilometres long, but only 50 kilometres wide at its narrowest point.

VIETNAM FACTS	
Capital city:	Hanoi
Land area:	331,041 square kilometres
Biggest rivers:	Mekong and Red River
Highest mountain:	Fan Si Pan, 3,143 metres

The main rivers, mountains and cities of Vietnam. ▶

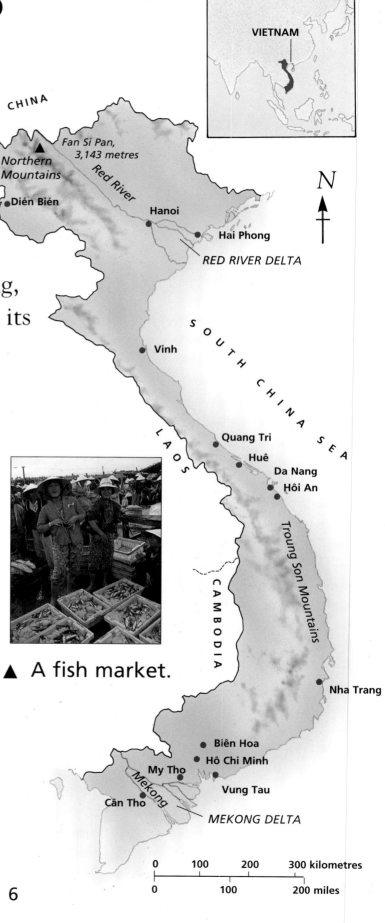

VIETNAM

N

CHINA

Fan Si Pan, 3,143 metres

Northern Mountains

Dién Bién

Red River

Hanoi

Hai Phong

RED RIVER DELTA

Vinh

SOUTH CHINA SEA

LAOS

Quang Tri

Huê

Da Nang

Hôi An

Troung Son Mountains

CAMBODIA

Nha Trang

Biên Hoa

Hô Chi Minh

My Tho

Vung Tau

Cân Tho

Mekong

MEKONG DELTA

▲ A fish market.

| 0 | 100 | 200 | 300 kilometres |
| 0 | 100 | | 200 miles |

▲ Paddy fields in the mountains near the border with Laos.

Three-quarters of Vietnam's landscape is made up of mountains or plateaus. Many small rivers start in the Troung Son Mountains. The biggest rivers, the Mekong and the Red River, have made fertile deltas at each end of the country.

VIETNAM'S LANDSCAPE

The Red River Delta and the Mekong Delta are the most important farming areas in Vietnam.

The Troung Son Mountains cover two-thirds of the country. They are covered with dense forests.

The Northern Mountains are where most of the country's mineral resources are found.

The coastal plain is a narrow, flat strip of land running down the country beside the coast.

VIETNAM'S FORESTS

Vast areas of Vietnam's forests have been lost over the past fifty years. US forces destroyed parts of them during the war. But most trees have been cut down by the Vietnamese, to use the wood for building, firewood and selling abroad.

LOSS OF FOREST	
Total area of forest	
1943	13.5 million hectares
1994	9.2 million hectares

Do Cuong, who works in a national park. ▼

When forests are cut down, rare plants and animals can die out. Soil is eroded more easily. In 1997, the government banned the sale of timber abroad to try to protect the forests. It started tree-planting projects to help the forests to grow back.

'Over 2,000 plants like this one can be used for food, medicine and wood products.'
– Do Cuong, from Cuc Phoung National Park.

Drizzling rain in northern Vietnam. ▶

	Hô Chi Minh		Hanoi	
	1	2	1	2
January	25	16	15	22
March	27	13	19	45
May	28	220	27	216
July	26	314	28	335
September	26	336	27	276
November	26	115	21	48

CLIMATE

Key:
1 = Average temperature in °Celsius
2 = Rain in mm

CLIMATE

Northern Vietnam can be very hot in the summer and bitterly cold in the winter. The end of winter brings months of drizzling rain, called 'rain dust'. In the summer, sometimes there are violent typhoons.

The south has a tropical climate. It is hot all year round. Evenings can be warm, with temperatures around 26 °Celsius. There is a dry season and a rainy season.

The weather can cause problems in Vietnam. In July to September 2000, terrible floods in the Mekong Delta killed about 100 people.

VIETNAM'S HISTORY

TIMELINE

111 BC to AD 938	China ruled Vietnam.
1887	Vietnam became a French colony.
1940 to 1945	Japan ruled Vietnam.
1945	France took over again.
1950	Country divided into North and South Vietnam.
1954	French defeated.
1964	US forces started bombing North Vietnam.
1973	Cease-fire signed. US forces left Vietnam.
1975	Vietnam became one country again.
1978	Vietnam invaded Cambodia.
1979	China attacked Vietnam.
1986	New economic policy brought in.
1995	Vietnam became a member of the South-East Asian Nations (ASEAN).

Vietnam was ruled by China for over 1,000 years. Chinese rule was often harsh, but the Vietnamese took on Chinese religions and education methods. They learnt to grow rice, too. But the Vietnamese wanted to be independent, and in the end they forced the Chinese out.

◄ A statue of the Goddess of Mercy. She is the most popular goddess in both the Chinese and Vietnamese cultures.

10

According to ancient traditions in Vietnam and China, the dead carry on living in the underworld. Living people have to give them everything they need. The living provide houses, servants, money, cars and clothes, all made out of paper. Everything is burned to transfer it to the underworld. Today, people in Vietnam keep these traditions, even if they do not believe that the dead live on.

▲ A funeral in Hanoi. All these gifts are made from paper.

In 1656, Vietnam conquered the kingdom of Champa, which is now in central Vietnam. Later, the lower Mekong Delta was taken over. This had been part of Cambodia.

The Temple of Literature University, which was founded in 1070. ▶

FRENCH RULE

Vietnam was ruled by France from 1887 until 1954, except for a time when Japan ruled from 1940 to 1945.

French rule was cruel. Before the French arrived, most people owned their own land. The French colonists took over a large area of the country. By the 1930s, 70 per cent of the Vietnamese were poor and had no land. Rubber plantations and mines were set up, but the Vietnamese were paid very low wages.

▲ A religious temple. In Vietnam, many people hold a mixture of Buddhist and Chinese religious beliefs.

Hô Chi Minh was president of North Vietnam from 1954 until his death. He led his country in a brave struggle against the French and forced them to leave Vietnam in 1954. His Communist government then led North Vietnam in the war with the USA. He became a Communist while living abroad, from 1911 to 1941. Hô Chi Minh's main aim was to free his country from foreign rule.

A portrait of Hô Chi Minh. ▶

Few Vietnamese did well under French rule. They were determined to throw out the French colonists and make their country independent.

▲ A memorial to Hô Chi Minh.

◀ The French brought bread to Vietnam. The Vietnamese still bake French bread.

THE VIETNAM WAR

In 1954, the Vietnamese drove out the French. But an even fiercer struggle began. Hô Chi Minh, Vietnam's leader, wanted to run the country as a Communist state. The USA did not want this to happen.

A US tank with a heavy gun, used during the war in Vietnam. ▼

Vietnam was divided into two states. North Vietnam was run by Hô Chi Minh's Communist government. South Vietnam was run by an anti-Communist government.

The USA supported South Vietnam in a war against North Vietnam. China and the USSR supported the North. The US government believed that its strong army would easily beat the Communists.

US planes dropped more bombs on Vietnam than had been used in Europe during the entire Second World War. Yet the more the USA bombed, the more Vietnamese joined the Communists.

◄ A Vietnamese woman watches her village going up in flames.

In 1968, during the Vietnamese New Year celebrations, the Communists attacked all the large cities in South Vietnam. The fighting was terrible. One battle, to take over the US military base at Khe Sanh, went on for 77 days. The US forces hit back hard and beat the Communists.

LIVING THROUGH THE WAR

Vu Thuy Bang was born in a village near Hai Phong, in North Vietnam. She had a normal childhood, working in the paddy fields in the morning and going to school in the afternoon.

When she was a teenager, the Vietnam War began. Bang can remember the US jets flying over her village. She was terrified. The village men, including her brothers, joined the North Vietnamese army. They went south to fight. Many did not return.

For a while, Bang had to leave school to work in the fields with her family. She read books while looking after the buffaloes. Later, after the US troops left in 1973, she went to work as a teacher in South Vietnam.

▲ Bang aged sixteen years. Her elder brother carried this photo for good luck during the fighting. He survived the war.

The terrible loss of life made the war very unpopular in the USA. Slowly, the US forces started to move out of Vietnam, leaving the South Vietnamese army to fight for itself. In 1975, the North Vietnamese army defeated the South. Vietnam became one again, this time under Vietnamese rule.

Bang outside her childhood home. ▼

This was a dangerous job because there was still fighting going on between the North and the South.

Bang survived the war, and today she lives a quiet life with her family in a small house in Hai Phong.

'The war broke my teenage dreams of studying and travelling. They were very hard years. But everybody in the village shared a feeling of determination. We wanted to serve our country.'
– Vu Thuy Bang, Hai Phong.

Bang at her house today, making lunch. ▼

CAMBODIA

Peace did not last long. In 1975, a brutal group called the Khmer Rouge took power in Cambodia. The group killed anyone who did not agree with it. About a million people were murdered, or died from hunger or disease. Cambodia also attacked Vietnam.

In 1978, Vietnam invaded Cambodia. Then China, which supported Cambodia, attacked Vietnam. Many countries, led by the USA, believed that Vietnam had caused the problem. They stopped trading with Vietnam.

◀ A minefield.

▼ A man making artificial legs for people who have walked on a mine.

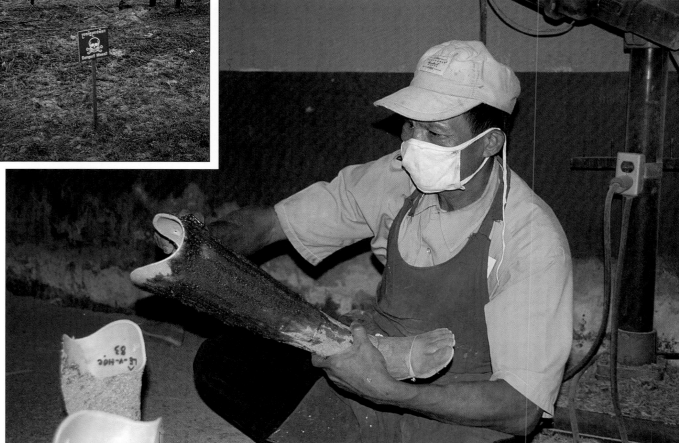

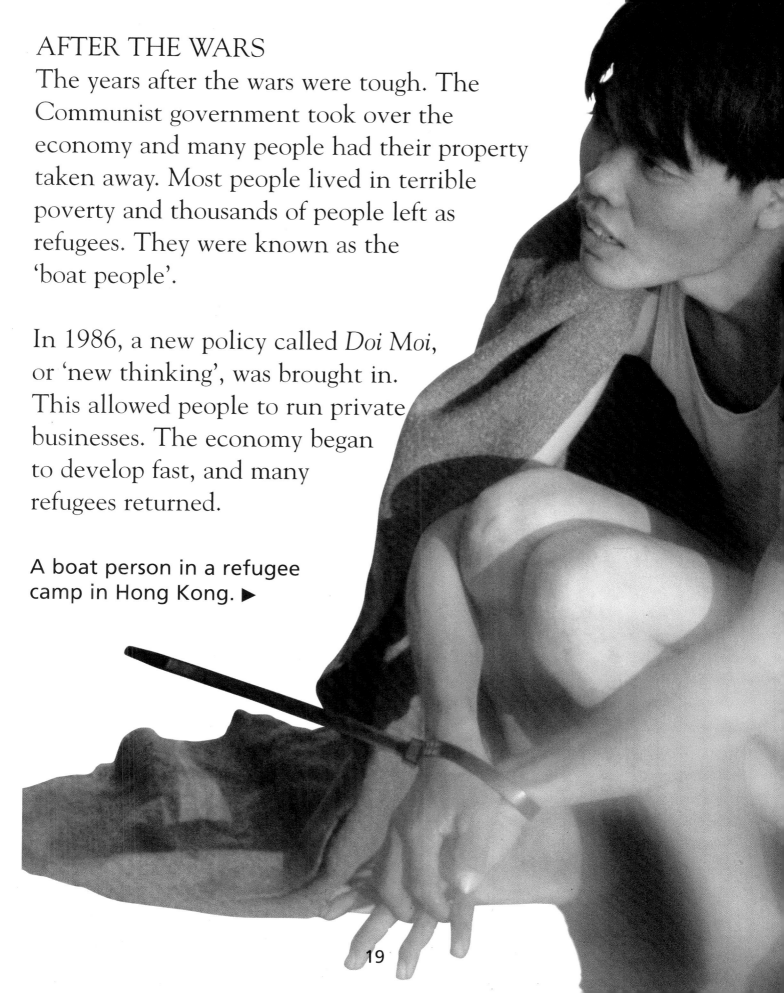

AFTER THE WARS

The years after the wars were tough. The Communist government took over the economy and many people had their property taken away. Most people lived in terrible poverty and thousands of people left as refugees. They were known as the 'boat people'.

In 1986, a new policy called *Doi Moi*, or 'new thinking', was brought in. This allowed people to run private businesses. The economy began to develop fast, and many refugees returned.

A boat person in a refugee camp in Hong Kong. ▶

THE PEOPLE

Vietnam has a population of almost 80 million people. This has more than doubled since 1960.

A large population can be a good thing. As the economy grows and the Vietnamese have more money, they will want to buy more goods. This means more foreign companies will come to Vietnam to sell goods. They will give jobs to local people.

On the other hand, parts of Vietnam are very overcrowded.

KEY:
Number of people per square kilometre

■ Over 5,000	■ 150–250
■ 1,000–5,000	■ 50–150
■ 500–1,000	■ 20–50
■ 250–500	□ Under 20

NUMBER OF PEOPLE

Number of people per square kilometre:

Bangladesh	873
Britain	242
USA	28
Vietnam	240

0   100   200   300 kilometres

0   100   200 miles

N

◀ This map shows how many people live in each part of Vietnam.

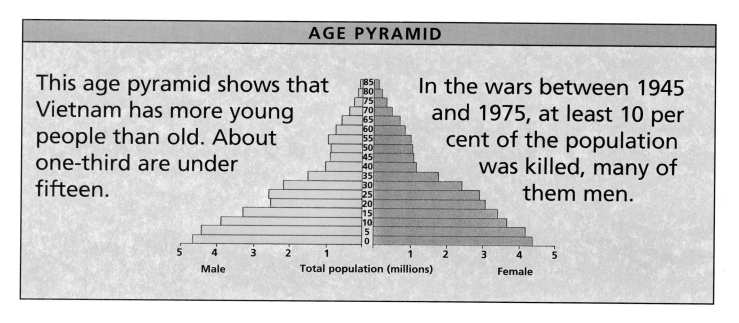

AGE PYRAMID

This age pyramid shows that Vietnam has more young people than old. About one-third are under fifteen.

In the wars between 1945 and 1975, at least 10 per cent of the population was killed, many of them men.

Male | Total population (millions) | Female

The cities in Vietnam are crowded. If all the people in England moved to live within the M25 motorway, the population would be as dense as the city of Hô Chi Minh.

Lack of space isn't the only problem caused by a high population. Because there are so many young people, it is hard for them all to find a job.

◄ Schoolboys in the countryside of the Red River Delta. About 81 per cent of the population live in the countryside. Parts of the countryside are crowded, too.

LIVING IN A BORDER VILLAGE

Ha Cong Guong is fifty-eight. He lives in a village close in the North-west Mountains. Guong is a Vietnamese-Thai.

Village life is changing in the mountains. Guong's wife still cooks over an open fire, but she can listen to the stereo while she works. The villagers now have TVs and fridges.

Many tourists visit the village. They like to see the old Thai culture. The women make traditional weavings to sell.

▲ Villagers make traditional Thai weavings to sell to tourists. ▶

Guong's family expect to stay in the village all their lives. But Guong hopes his grand-daughter will go to Hanoi University.

'Many mountain villages are poor. Visits from tourists help to raise our standard of living.' – Ha Cong Guong, from Mai Chau village, North-west Mountains.

FAMILY LIFE

Looking after the family is important to the Vietnamese. Usually, grandparents live with their children and grandchildren.

Most Vietnamese families get up at about 5 a.m. They sit on mats on the floor to eat a breakfast of noodle soup with rice or bread. Then they go to school or work. At midday, the whole family returns for a lunch of rice, fish and vegetables.

▼ A Vietnamese family outside their house, sitting on their motorbike.

'I have six sisters and one brother. Today I have my own family and many friends. I am lucky.' – Vo Thi Sinh, in Vinh city.

In the afternoon, the adults return to work while children study at home. After supper, there is time for playing, watching TV or visiting friends.

▲ Vo Thi Sinh making tea. In Vietnam, visitors are always served tea.

◄ Families sit on mats on the floor to eat. They use chopsticks instead of knives and forks.

ETHNIC GROUPS

There are 54 ethnic groups in Vietnam. They make up 13 per cent of the population. Most of them live in the less-crowded mountain areas.

The Chinese live at the centre of modern life. Half of them live in Cholon, the Chinatown of Hô Chi Minh City. The Chinese have always worked in business in Vietnam.

After 1975, the Communist government did not trust them. In about 1979, many left as refugees. Things are better now, and the Chinese have returned to manage businesses.

MAJOR ETHNIC GROUPS		
Ethnic group	Where they live	Percentage of Population
Tay-Thai	North-west Mountains	4.8%
Mon-Khmer	Mekong Delta, Cambodian border and Central Vietnam	2.6%
Chinese	Hô Chi Minh City, Mekong Delta, southern coast and north-east Vietnam	1.5%

FARMING AND FISHING

Although Vietnam is the second-largest exporter of rice in the world, people in some areas are short of food. Nearly half the children under five years old do not get enough to eat.

The country is so mountainous that only a quarter of it can be farmed. Farmers have to make the best use of the land they have. They dig irrigation systems and build terraces so that more land can be used.

The Red River Delta and the Mekong Delta are the most important farming areas. Over half of Vietnam's food is grown there.

▲ Few farms have machinery. This field is being irrigated by hand.

MAIN CROPS, 1999 (TONNES)	
Rice (paddy)	29 million
Sugar-cane	14 million
Vegetables	5 million
Coconuts	1 million

RICE

▲ A man sifting out rice grains. Behind him, farmers are using a machine worked by pedals to sift the rice.

The shape of Vietnam is said to look like a bamboo pole with a rice basket at each end – the Mekong Delta and the Red River Delta. These are the main areas for growing rice.

Nearly 80 per cent of food grown in Vietnam is rice. It can be boiled, fried or made into noodles. When people cannot afford to buy meat, fish or vegetables, they just eat rice.

Fresh green vegetables being sold in Hoi An market. ▶

▲ Fruit and vegetables being taken to a floating market in the Mekong Delta.

OTHER CROPS

Vietnamese farmers grow lots of other crops, too. There are many kinds of vegetables, and fruit such as pineapples, mangos and oranges. People grow crops such as tea, coffee, rubber, soy beans and peanuts mostly for export. Highland areas, which are not good for growing rice, are used for these other crops.

◄ Chickens being taken to the market by motorbike. Few people can afford to eat chicken in Vietnam.

SELLING ABROAD

Vietnam has old machinery. This makes it hard to produce goods quickly and easily. For example, most countries use 12–13 tonnes of sugar cane to make one tonne of sugar. But in Vietnam, 20 tonnes are used. This makes it difficult for Vietnamese farmers to make much money selling their goods abroad.

DONGS PER FARM WORKER (THOUSANDS)

	1,198
	1,031–1,079
	793–846
	675–756
	538–603
	413–500
	262–392

◄ This map shows the value of farm production per farm worker in Vietnam. The Dong is the currency (money) in Vietnam.

0	100	200	300 kilometres
0		100	200 miles

N

FARM ANIMALS

Buffalo, oxen, pigs and poultry are the most common farm animals. Buffalo and oxen are used for work in the fields.

FISHING

The Vietnamese eat lots of fish. With its long coastline and many rivers, Vietnam is a good place for fishing. There is a growing export industry selling frozen and tinned fish abroad.

FISH SAUCE
Fish sauce is a typical Vietnamese flavouring. It is made by putting small fish in water with salt for nine months. Then the liquid is mixed with more water, sugar, lime, chilli and garlic. The sauce is eaten with spring rolls, meat or fish. It is also used in cooking.

The early-morning fish market in Da Nang. ▼

Unfortunately, the growth of other industries such as mining means there is more pollution in Vietnam's seas.

Overfishing is another problem. In some places, fishermen use nets that catch young fish, as well as bigger ones. They do not leave enough fish to breed, so there are fewer fish.

Fishing in a canal in the Red River Delta. ▼

A boy takes fuel out to the fishing boats in Long Hai. ▼

ECONOMIC CHANGE

Things are changing fast in Vietnam. It is one of the fastest-growing economies in South-East Asia.

From 1975, the government ran all the industries in Vietnam. But this was not a good way of developing industry. In 1986, a new policy called *Doi Moi* was started.

Doi Moi meant that people could set up their own businesses. Foreign companies were allowed to put money into businesses in Vietnam. Soon, thousands of small businesses, from market stalls to clothing factories, were set up.

◀ A stall selling CDs in Hô Chi Minh City. Many people can now afford to buy luxuries such as CDs.

◄ Dam is seventeen years old. She helps her mother's business, making flower arrangements for funerals.

Growing Vietnam's economy is a difficult job. It is still one of the poorest countries in the world because of many years of war. Many companies that used to be helped by the government have closed down.

Unemployment is still a problem, especially among young people. The benefits of *Doi Moi* have not yet spread to the whole population.

GROSS DOMESTIC PRODUCT (GDP), 1998		
	GDP per person (US$)	Growth rate
China	$750	9.2%
Japan	$32,350	1.1%
United Kingdom	$21,410	1.6%
USA	$29,240	1.8%
Vietnam	$350	6.1%

Vietnam is poor, but its economy is growing faster than many richer countries.

INDUSTRY

In 1999, only 12 per cent of the workforce worked in industry, but they produced 35 per cent of Vietnam's total wealth.

In the north, mining and heavy industry such as making machinery are important.

VIHN CITY

Vinh is a large city in north-central Vietnam. It is one of the poorest cities in Vietnam.

In the last ten years, new industries have been set up in Vinh, such as a textile (cloth-making) factory. Its cotton goods are sold to several countries, such as France, Germany and Japan. A seafood company sells frozen fish to Japan, Hong Kong and Taiwan.

◀ Workers at Vinh's seafood factory.

Most of the raw materials that are needed are found in Vietnam's Northern Mountains.

The south has more light industry, such as food processing. Many industries are trying to sell their products abroad.

A large brewery was set up in Vinh in 1985 and run by the government. Now it is run as a private company. The brewery makes high-quality beer.

A big building project is planned in the city. By 2020, it will provide housing for the growing population. All Vinh's new industries will be in a brand-new industrial zone.

▲ Making beer in Vinh's brewery.

The dyeing hall in the textile factory. ▶

People and goods travelling on a river ferry. ▶

TRANSPORT

Travel in Vietnam is slow. Most people use bicycles or motorbikes. Few people own cars, so travel around the country is usually by bus or train.

The transport systems are poor in Vietnam. Roads, bridges and railways were badly damaged during the wars, and rebuilding has been slow. Vietnam needs to improve its road and rail systems to help it get richer.

The main road in Vietnam, National Highway One, carries buffaloes and bicycles. It also carries large trucks and a few fast cars. Only 15 per cent of Vietnam's roads have a hard surface.

'The new highway between Hanoi and Hô Chi Minh City will help us to develop our villages.' – Ho Xuan Hung, the Chairman of the People's Committee of Nghe An.

◄ Some people use the main road for drying rice.

There is just one main railway line in Vietnam, between Hanoi and Hô Chi Minh City. The express trains run at only 40 kilometres an hour and the journey takes over 40 hours. The government plans to improve Vietnam's railways. By 2020, there should be high-speed trains linking all the major cities.

MOTORBIKES

Although few Vietnamese can afford a car, more and more people are buying motorbikes. In Hô Chi Minh City, there are about 1 million motorbikes. They cause air pollution, so people have to cover their faces as protection.

◄ Advertising is increasing in Vietnam. This is a foreign company's billboard.

FOREIGN INVESTMENT

Singapore, Taiwan and other East-Asian countries have put money into Vietnamese businesses. Some Western companies have come to Vietnam to sell their goods and set up factories. In 1994, the USA began trading with Vietnam again.

But sometimes foreign companies have been put off. For example, in the mid-1990s, the government banned foreign magazines and the use of English in adverts.

New offices and houses are needed for foreign companies moving to Hô Chi Minh City. ►

The rules have now been changed, and it is easier for foreign companies to work in Vietnam. In 2000, it seemed likely that they would be putting a lot of money into businesses there.

The Vietnamese like to work for foreign companies because they pay better wages. But some of these businesses treat Vietnamese workers badly.

FOREIGN INVESTORS IN VIETNAM, 1998	
Country	Total Investment (millions of US$)
Singapore	224
Taiwan	194
Japan	541
Hong Kong	105

TOYS

When Tran Toung Nhi was a child, she had to make her own toys from whatever she could find at home. Now, there are companies in Vietnam selling toys made in factories.

Tran is a manager for an international company called Lego. Toys made by Lego are very expensive for Vietnamese people because they are sold at Western prices.

'Some customers are rich, but others are ordinary people who have saved money to buy a small box of Lego.' – Tran Toung Nhi, from Hô Chi Minh City.

◄ The Cu Chi tunnels, near Hô Chi Minh City. A guide is showing tourists where Communist soldiers once hid.

NUMBER OF TOURISTS	
1992	400,000
1994	1,000,000
1997	1,700,000

INCOME FROM HOTELS AND RESTAURANTS			
(figures are in billions of Dongs)			
1993	5,119	1996	9,776
1994	6,125	1997	11,307
1995	8,625	1998	12,404

TOURISM

The government is encouraging the tourist industry in Vietnam. There is plenty for tourists to see. Vietnam has beautiful scenery, unspoilt beaches and historical places of interest. Many come to see the battlefields where the Vietnam War was fought.

Tourists are usually welcomed by the Vietnamese, who like meeting foreigners.

They like to practise their English, or make money working with the visitors. An English-speaking tour guide can easily earn in one day what a teacher earns in a week.

▲ Many young Vietnamese come to downtown Hô Chi Minh City to chat to tourists.

THE PERFUME PAGODA

The Perfume Pagoda, south of Hanoi, is actually a group of pagodas, shrines and caves tucked away along a mountain path. For hundreds of years, pilgrims have travelled there in March and April.

Over the past fifteen years, salespeople have begun to offer food and services to the travellers. There are even karaoke bars.

Unemployed people come to beg, too. Some have entered the spirit of competition. They use loudspeakers to raise their voices above the other beggars.

A musician trying to make money near the Perfume Pagoda. ▼

A POOR COUNTRY?

▲ Cycling home from school.

When you look at the amount of wealth that each person produces, Vietnam is one of the poorest countries in the world.

But when you look at other things, such as literacy rates and life expectancy, Vietnam does better than more wealthy countries. For example, Brazil's wealth per person is over thirteen times higher than Vietnam's, but its life expectancy is almost one year lower.

SCHOOLS

Vietnamese children go to school six days a week. They often have private lessons on Sunday, too.

Under *Doi Moi*, the government spends less money on education. Parents have to pay towards their children's schooling, so some children have had to leave school.

0   100   200   300 km

0   100   200 miles

N

Percentage of population over 10 years

- 84–92
- 77–83
- 67–69
- 58–60
- 48

This map shows the percentage of population over 10 years of age who can read, in the different parts of Vietnam. ▶

HEALTH

People in Vietnam suffer from poverty and lack of food. So they are more likely to become seriously ill than people in rich countries. In the past, health care was free in Vietnam. Now, all but the poorest people have to pay for their treatment.

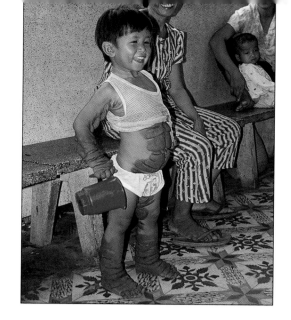

▲ A child with elephantiasis, a disease spread by mosquitoes.

◄ Foreign aid has helped to buy ambulances like these to bring people to medical centres.

QUALITY OF LIFE (1998)	
Life expectancy	67.4 years
Percentage of people over 15 years who can read and write	92.9%
Percentage of people in schools and colleges	63%
Number of children who die under the age of 5 years	42 per 1,000 births

THE FUTURE

▲ A boat carrying bricks on the Red River Delta. More people in the countryside can afford brick houses now.

Vietnam is an amazing country. Although it was bombed and destroyed by war, the country recovered rapidly. Then in 1996–97 there was an economic crisis in South-East Asia. By 1999 things had got better. Now Vietnam is getting richer.

Since *Doi Moi*, a few Vietnamese have become very rich. They can afford to buy modern cars and luxury homes. Others are earning enough money to be able to buy colour televisions and stereos.

◄ This man runs his own business selling balloons.

The gap between the rich and the poor has grown. Some people are unemployed, while many farmers no longer have enough land to grow their food.

But most people feel that life has got better. They are free to work for themselves instead of for the government. They run their own businesses and farm their own land. The Vietnamese have high hopes of a bright future, free from war and poverty.

'I am only twenty, but Vietnam has changed a lot in my lifetime. I hope to have a career in international banking.' – Linh, from Hanoi.

GLOSSARY

Aid Money that is given by a wealthy country to help a poorer country.

Colony A land ruled by another country.

Communist A person who supports Communism, a system where a country's wealth is owned by the whole population, controlled by the state.

Crops Plants that are grown by people to use.

Delta A fan-shaped area of land where a river splits into channels as it flows into the sea.

Economy The wealth and resources belonging to a country.

Eroded Worn away.

Ethnic groups Groups of people with a common culture.

Export To sell good abroad.

Gross Domestic Product (GDP) The value of all the goods and services made in a country during one year.

Independence Free from foreign rule.

Irrigation The watering of crops using channels or pipes.

Life expectancy The number of years people can expect to live.

Literacy rates The percentage of a country's population who can read and write.

Mine A bomb placed underground that goes off when someone moves over it.

Overfishing Catching too many fish so that the fish cannot breed quickly enough to replace those that have been caught.

Paddy fields Fields covered in water, where rice is grown.

Plantations Large farms.

Plateaus Large areas of flat land in the mountains or above sea-level.

Population The people living in a place or country.

Refugees People who leave their own country in a time of war, disaster or other danger.

Resources Supplies of things such as oil or water that people need.

Terraces Flat areas cut into a slope so that crops can be grown in hilly places.

Tropical Belonging to the Tropics, the zone on either side of the Equator, between the Tropics of Cancer and Capricorn.

Typhoons Violent storms, with winds circling round very fast.

TOPIC WEB

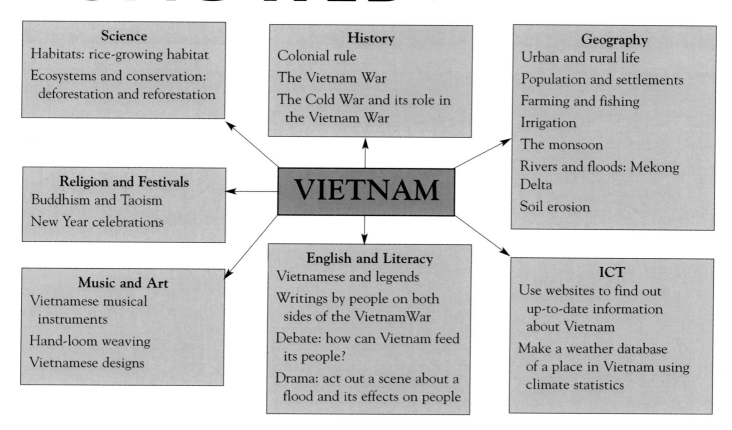

Science
Habitats: rice-growing habitat
Ecosystems and conservation: deforestation and reforestation

History
Colonial rule
The Vietnam War
The Cold War and its role in the Vietnam War

Geography
Urban and rural life
Population and settlements
Farming and fishing
Irrigation
The monsoon
Rivers and floods: Mekong Delta
Soil erosion

Religion and Festivals
Buddhism and Taoism
New Year celebrations

VIETNAM

Music and Art
Vietnamese musical instruments
Hand-loom weaving
Vietnamese designs

English and Literacy
Vietnamese and legends
Writings by people on both sides of the Vietnam War
Debate: how can Vietnam feed its people?
Drama: act out a scene about a flood and its effects on people

ICT
Use websites to find out up-to-date information about Vietnam
Make a weather database of a place in Vietnam using climate statistics

FINDING OUT MORE

BOOKS TO READ
A Family from Vietnam by Simon Scoones
(Hodder Wayland, 1998)
Postcards from Vietnam by Denise Allard
(Zoë Books, 1996)
World Focus: Vietnam by Pat Simmons
(Heinemann, 1995)

You can also find out about Vietnam from travel guide books, such as the *Lonely Planet Guide* and the *Rough Guide to Vietnam*.

ORGANIZATIONS AND WEBSITES
Asia Observer – Vietnam
www.asiaobserver.com/vietnam.htm
News and background information on Vietnam.

ActionAid works in Vietnam on farming, health and water projects.
Tel: 020 7561 7561

Investigating the Vietnam War
www.spartacus.schoolnet.co.uk/vietnam.html
A website for schools with excellent material.

Lonely Planet – Destination Vietnam
www.lonelyplanet.com/dest/sea/vietnam.htm

Oxfam Cool Planet
www.oxfam.org.uk/coolplanet/index.html
Good web pages on Vietnam.

INDEX

Page numbers in **bold**
show pictures as well
as text.